Your World

Germs

Addition and Subtraction

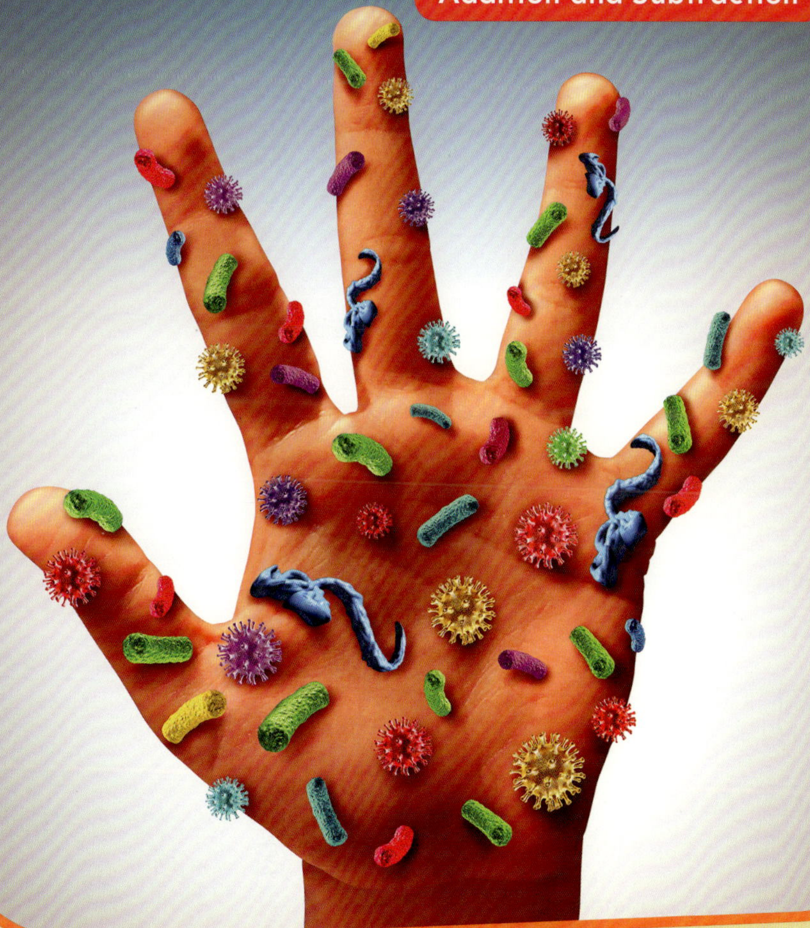

Dona Herweck Rice

Consultants

Colene Van Brunt
Math Coach
Hillsborough County Public Schools

Publishing Credits

Rachelle Cracchiolo, M.S.Ed., *Publisher*
Conni Medina, M.A.Ed., *Managing Editor*
Dona Herweck Rice, *Series Developer*
Emily R. Smith, M.A.Ed., *Series Developer*
Diana Kenney, M.A.Ed., NBCT, *Content Director*
June Kikuchi, *Content Director*
Susan Daddis, M.A.Ed., *Editor*
Karen Malaska, M.Ed., *Editor*
Kevin Panter, *Senior Graphic Designer*

Image Credits: all images from iStock and/or Shutterstock.

Library of Congress Cataloging-in-Publication Data

Names: Rice, Dona, author.
Title: Your world : germs / Dona Herweck Rice.
Other titles: Germs
Description: Huntington Beach, CA : Teacher Created Materials, [2018] | Audience: K to grade 3. | Includes index. |
Identifiers: LCCN 2017054970 (print) | LCCN 2017060009 (ebook) | ISBN 9781480759794 (eBook) | ISBN 9781425856854 (pbk.)
Subjects: LCSH: Bacteria--Juvenile literature.
Classification: LCC QR74.8 (ebook) | LCC QR74.8 .R54 2018 (print) | DDC 579.3--dc23
LC record available at https://lccn.loc.gov/2017054970

Teacher Created Materials
5301 Oceanus Drive
Huntington Beach, CA 92649-1030
www.tcmpub.com

ISBN 978-1-4258-5685-4

Printed in China WAI002

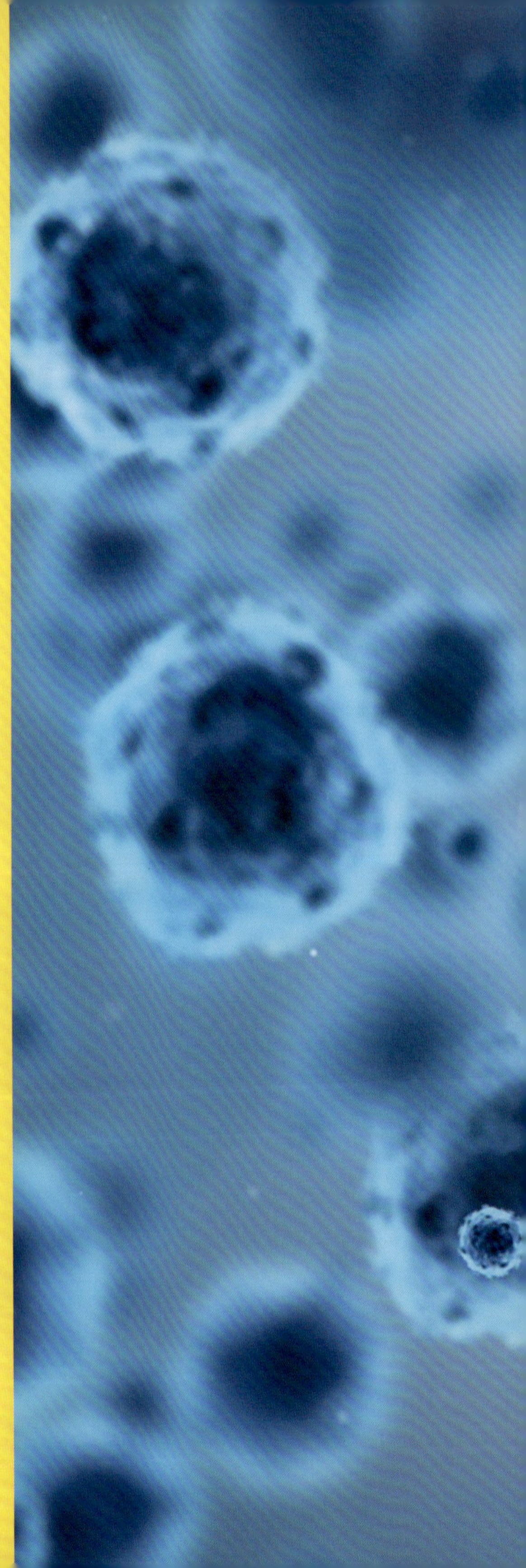

Table of Contents

Little Sneaks

They are all around! They are on you. They are inside you, too.

What are they? Germs!

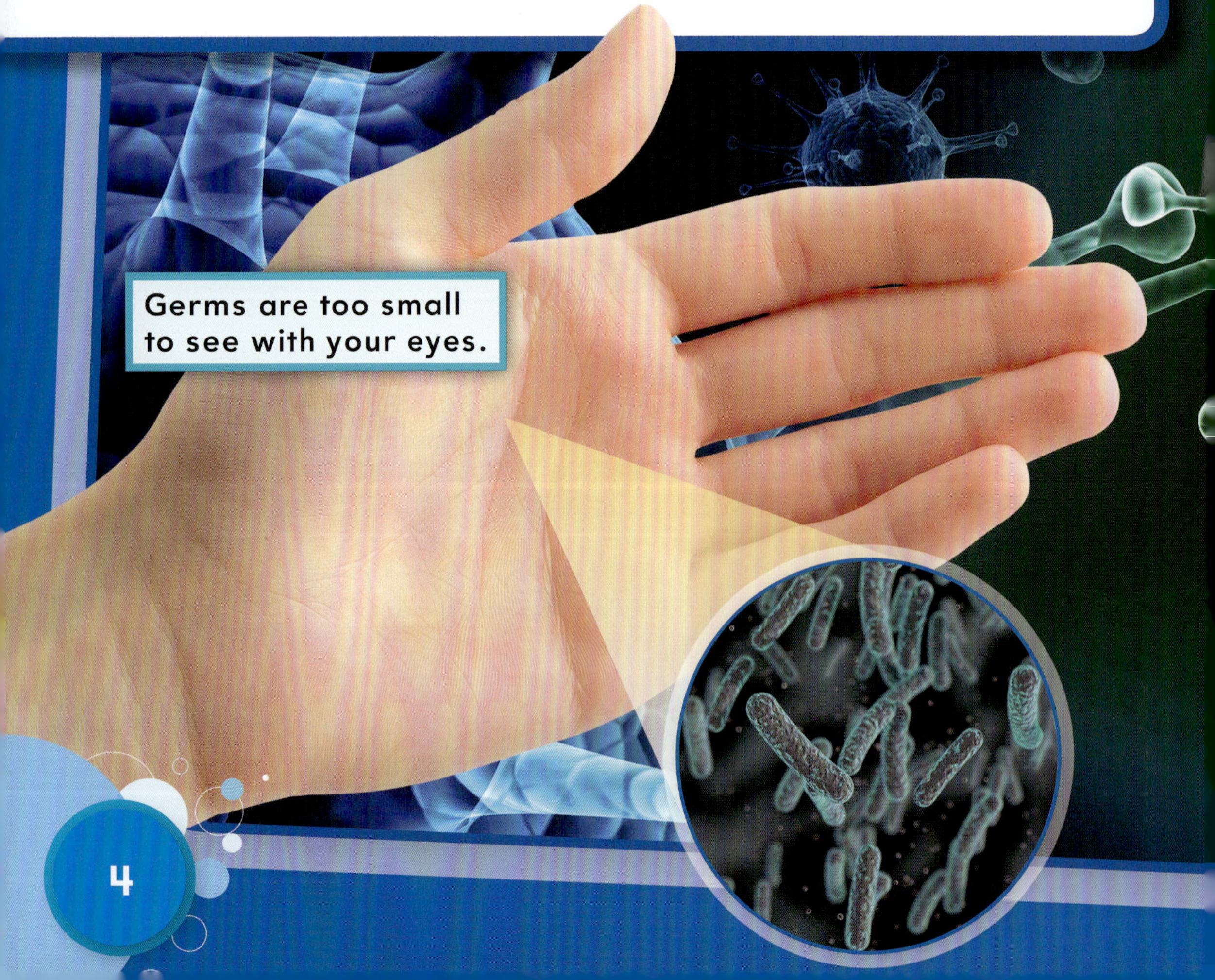

Germs are too small to see with your eyes.

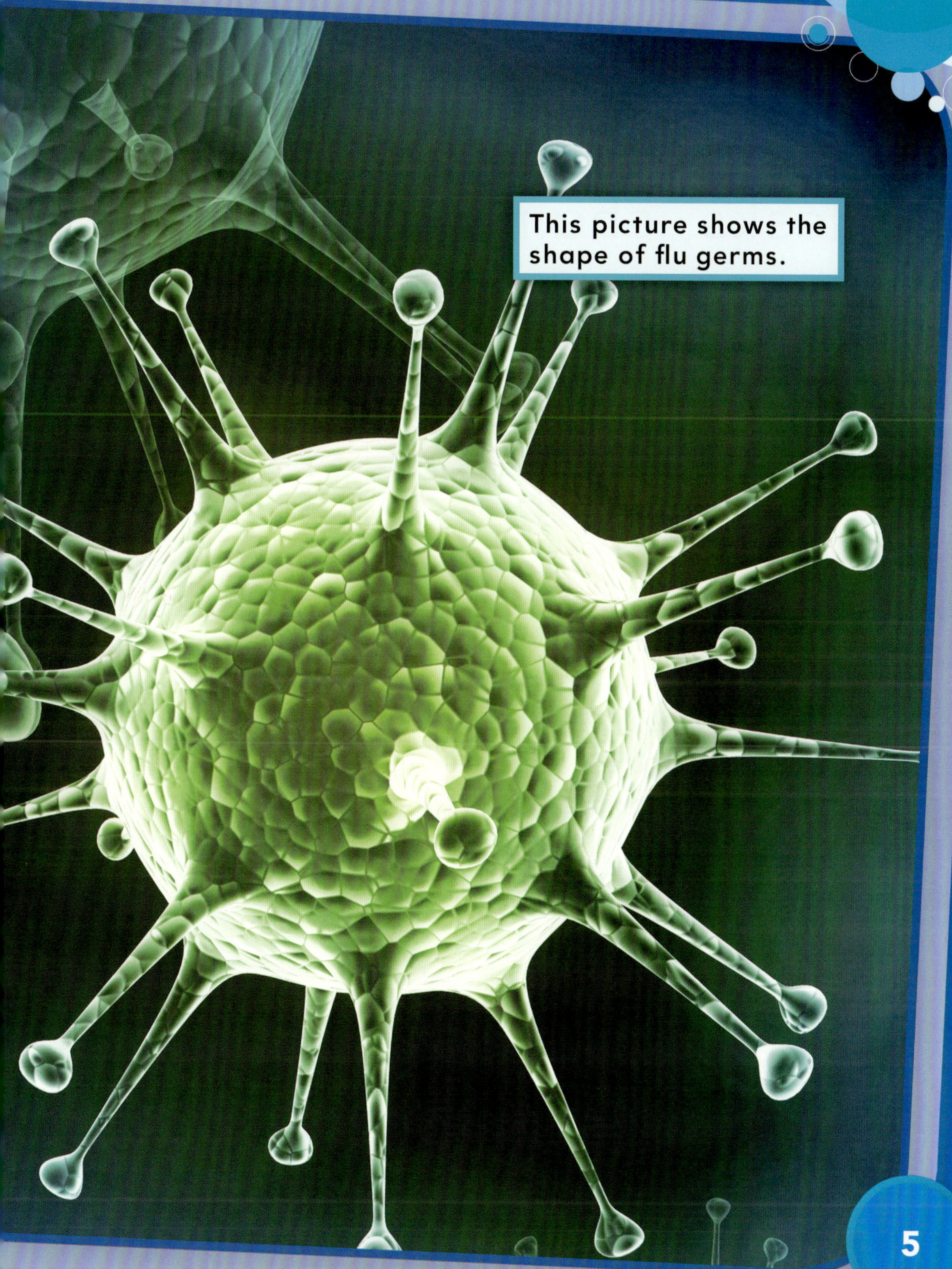

This picture shows the shape of flu germs.

Germs are tiny and **sneaky**. They are on desks, chairs, and pencils. They are everywhere. But it can be hard to tell.

What Germs Do

You cannot see germs because they are too small. You need a **microscope**. You might use this tool when you learn about germs.

Let's Do Math!

Mr. Lee teaches science. He has 16 microscopes. He buys 10 more. How many microscopes does he have now? Solve with a number line.

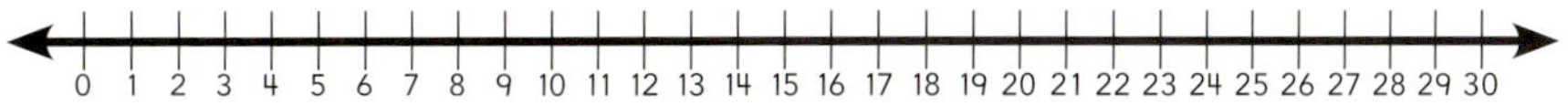

Germs can make you sick.

They can cause colds, fevers, and stomachaches.

Not all germs hurt you. Some germs help. They help your body use food.

This girl eats yogurt, which has good germs.

They also help get rid of **waste**.

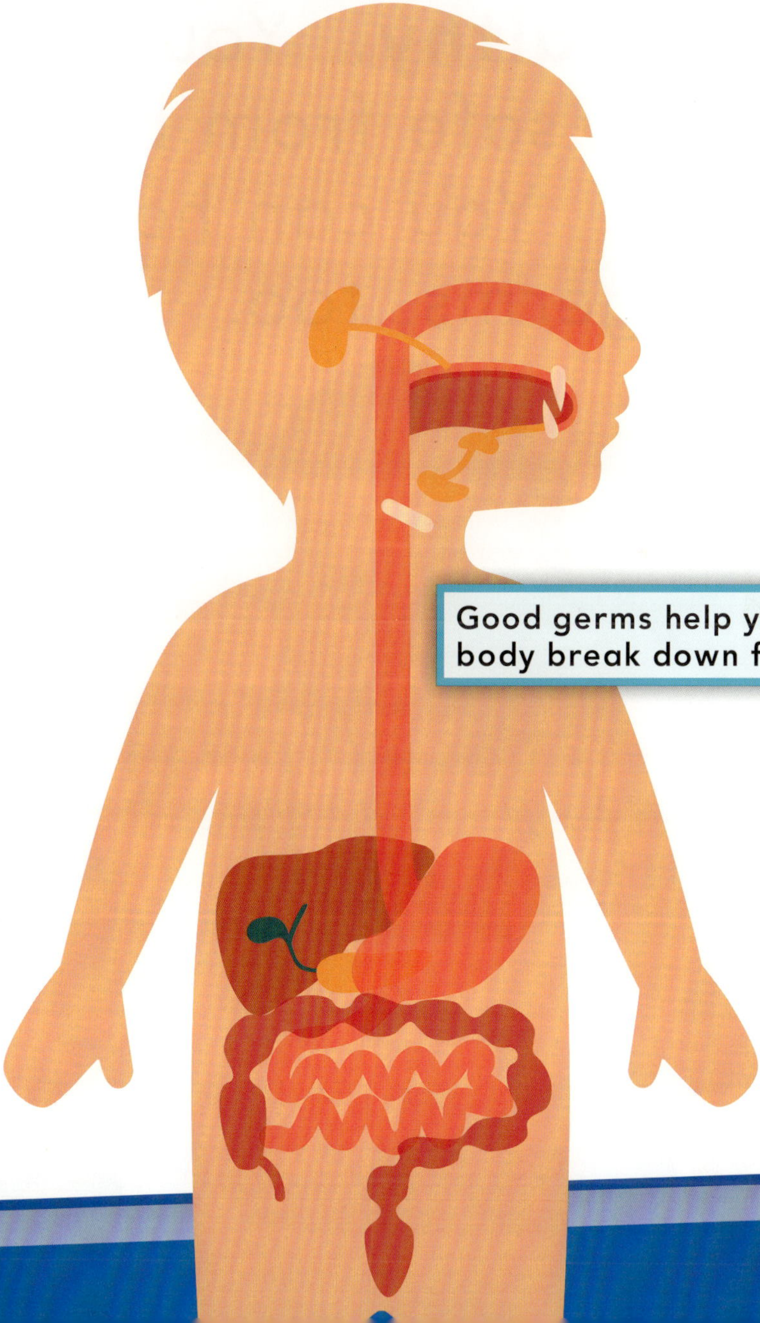

Good germs help your body break down food.

No Germs!

You can help your body stay **healthy**. You can keep it safe from bad germs. You can help it fight germs, too.

Wash your hands before you eat. Wash after you use the bathroom.

Use soap and warm water when you wash.

Cover your mouth when you **cough**. Cover your nose and mouth when you **sneeze**. Use a tissue or the inside of your elbow. Then, wash your hands again.

Goodbye, germs!

Let's Do Math!

Rosa has 60 tissues. She has a cold and uses 20 tissues. How many tissues does she have left? Solve with groups of 10.

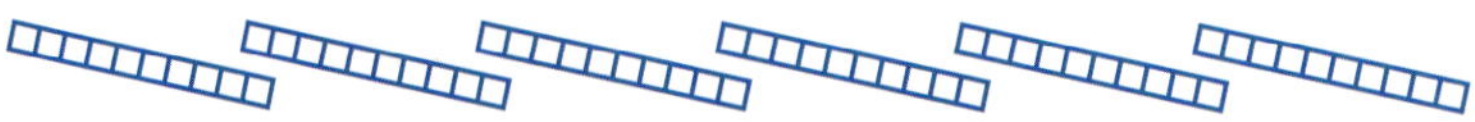

This girl covers her mouth and nose while sneezing.

Problem Solving

A class pretends that glitter specks are germs. They put the "germs" on their hands. They watch the germs spread. At the end of the day, there are...

- 31 germs on a pencil
- 47 germs on a chair
- 82 germs on a desk

Solve the problems with the hundreds chart.

1. Pia's hands are covered with germs. She spreads 10 more germs onto each item. How many germs are on each item now?

2. Ty wipes 30 germs from the desk after Pia leaves. How many germs are left?

1	2	3	4	5	6	7	8	9	10
11	12	13	14	15	16	17	18	19	20
21	22	23	24	25	26	27	28	29	30
31	32	33	34	35	36	37	38	39	40
41	42	43	44	45	46	47	48	49	50
51	52	53	54	55	56	57	58	59	60
61	62	63	64	65	66	67	68	69	70
71	72	73	74	75	76	77	78	79	80
81	82	83	84	85	86	87	88	89	90
91	92	93	94	95	96	97	98	99	100

Glossary

cough—to force air up through the throat and out the mouth in a short, noisy burst

healthy—not sick

microscope—a tool that makes tiny objects bigger and easier to see

sneaky—not seen or known by others

sneeze—to force air through and out the nose in a short, noisy burst

waste—substance that is not needed or wanted

Index

Answer Key

Let's Do Math!

page 9:

26 microscopes

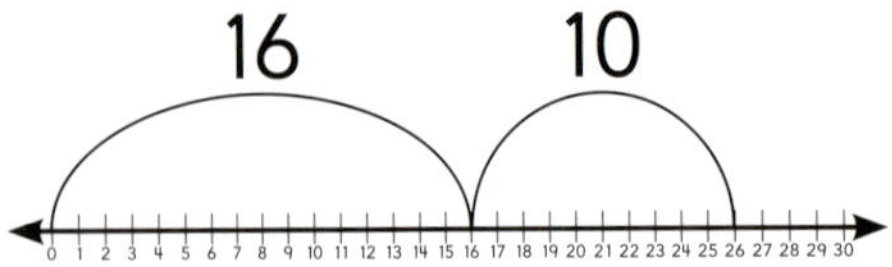

page 18:

40 tissues

Problem Solving

1. pencil: 41 germs; chair: 57 germs; desk: 92 germs

2. 62 germs